Contents

1.1 What are the stories about?

Work with another student. Read the Contents page. Then answer the questions.
Write the numbers of the stories.

1 ☐ Which story do you think the scene on the front cover comes from?

2 Which story do you think is about:

a ☐ a soldier who lost his sight?

b ☐ an old lady with a lot of money?

c ☐ mysterious events beside water?

d ☐ terror from the sky?

e ☐ a terrible experience on the road?

f ☐ two engineers and a problem with water?

1.2 What happens first?

1 On page 1, look at the title, the sentences in *italics* below it and the picture.
Look at the picture on page 5. What do you think? Circle the best answer.

1 The dream in the title will be about ... .

    a an accident   **b** murder   **c** a family holiday

2 The story-teller is ... in the car on page 1.

    a the man   **b** the woman   **c** the boy

3 The family car will ... .

    a crash and kill the family   **b** crash and kill another driver

    c not crash and nobody will be hurt

2 Which road could be in:

    a ☐ the United States?   **b** ☐ France?   **c** ☐ Britain?

The Dream

Frank Tilsley

Even if dreams can show us the future, this dream did not make sense.
Must I never pass a lorry on a clear road?

Can a dream show us the future and give us the opportunity of changing it? It is hard to believe. If we can see the future in a dream, then surely the future already exists. If it does, then we are not free to act in the ways we wish to; we are not responsible for our own lives.

Before I tell you the dream, I must explain a little about the context. It was the summer of four years ago, and I was driving my family back from Italy through the south of France. My son had not yet learned to drive, my daughter was too young, and my wife doesn't drive at all. I had been at the wheel for the best part of three weeks. Perhaps I was tired; perhaps I could think of nothing except cars. We spent the night of the dream in a town called Tain l'Hermitage.

Now I'll tell you the dream. I was sitting in a big, powerful, cream-coloured car, and I was driving at high speed through the country. I was coming to a bend in the road, and in front of me there was a very large lorry.

My foot reached out towards the **brake**, but it could not find it. I looked down: there was no brake! Worse: my hands held empty air. There was no wheel for them to hold. There were no controls of any kind. Already we were almost into the back of the lorry.

I shouted in fear. Then I heard a calm voice coming from my left, and I turned my head. A stranger was sitting there. He was a cheerful man of about forty. He was wearing an expensive shirt, and on his head he had a red hat. I couldn't understand what he said; he spoke very quickly in French, and my own French is not very good. I didn't, in fact, care what he said. My eyes were on his clean, fat hands, which were holding the wheel. This car had its wheel on the left. He, not I, was in control.

We drove safely round the bend. He turned the wheel slightly to place the car in the middle of the road. He was going to pass the lorry. The road stretched straight ahead. It was bright in the sunlight and it was quite empty. Only one other person was in sight; a woman was sitting outside a small house with white walls, and this house was almost exactly ahead of us. She was sitting by a table putting some flowers in pots. She wanted to sell us some, and waved them at us.

This sight, for some reason, filled me with a terrible fear. The flowers made me think of death and our final resting place.

At this moment we were level with the lorry and ready to pass it, but then the lorry began to turn away from the side of the road, towards our car. It appeared that the driver was doing this on purpose. The stranger by my side shouted loudly and tried to move out of the way. There was a terrible noise from the back of the car, and then an explosion. The earth seemed to turn over, and the noise of flames burned in my ears. At that point I woke up in fear.

I was very worried by this dream, and could not sleep again. It seemed to have a message, and I wanted to explain it.

Even if dreams can show us the future, this dream did not make sense. Must I never pass a lorry on a clear road? The road to Paris is always filled with very large lorries. Most of them come up from Marseilles, and I always have to pass them when the road is clear; I can't drive slowly behind them for ever. No, this was not the meaning of the dream. At its heart was some kind of fear. I had to recognize my fear, and then I could forget all about it.

I thought about my driving during the last three weeks. I tried to remember all the lorries and all the small white houses. I thought of all the cars which were

brake /breɪk/ (n) the part of a vehicle that makes it go more slowly or stop

painted cream. I remembered nothing of any great interest. I had imagined that the road in the dream must be in France; it was long, empty and straight. But then I remembered that we had passed the lorry on the right. So the dream was about a road in England; in England all cars keep to the left. Immediately, I remembered something.

Two years before this, I was travelling in the north of England. An American and I were making some radio programmes. He had brought his car from America, and of course the driver sat on the left side. The brakes and other controls were also on the left, but the colour of his car was not cream.

The American was a careless driver, and often passed other cars against my advice. Remember that I was in a better position to see: I was sitting on the right. Once, just after Nottingham, he played 'chicken'.

You probably know about 'chicken'; it is a game that is played on the roads. It is becoming more and more popular in America, because long journeys are often very dull. You just move your car into the middle of the road and stay there. When another car appears, it comes towards you in the middle of the road. The driver who turns away is the chicken. Quite often neither driver turns away.

I expressed my displeasure at this game in language that the American could not fail to understand. We did not play it again, but it had probably left its mark on my mind. So then, when I was asleep, I experienced it all again in a dream. I also remembered something else while I was having breakfast. When we played 'chicken', it was an uncommonly windy day. We stopped at Chesterfield, and the American bought a hat. It was a black hat, not a red one, but in dreams details are not always exact. After this I forgot about the dream until the afternoon.

The big French lorries often play their own game. They stay in the middle of the road, and you can't pass them. You have to stay behind them. Sometimes you have to follow them for endless kilometres, although the roads are almost completely empty.

This afternoon we were following a large vehicle which was making terrible noises. When I blew my **horn**, the driver moved to the side of the road, but it was the wrong side. He was driving along on the left, instead of keeping to the right. There was enough space on the right for me to pass him. But to do that would be wrong. So I just followed him for a few kilometres and I told myself not to pass him.

I considered the situation from every point of view. I could certainly turn my car more quickly than he could turn his lorry. It was a very big, heavy lorry. Could I, perhaps, pass him quickly on the right before he could do anything? If he turned to the right, though, he could easily kill us all. He probably wanted a

horn /hɔːn/ (n) the part of a car that you push to make a warning sound

bit of fun, but he might want an accident. If he killed us, nobody would say it was his fault; the law would be on his side.

The road ahead was quite empty, and went on for many kilometres. I drove more slowly until some distance separated us. Then I increased my speed as much as I could. I drove towards that empty space beside the lorry. My car was moving at about 110 kilometres an hour.

The front of my car was almost level with the back of the lorry. Then I saw something that knocked the breath out of my body. On the grass beside the road a woman was sitting outside a small white house with a table of flowers!

For the first time in my life I changed my mind while I was preparing to pass another vehicle. My foot went down hard on the brake. The car rocked from side to side. From behind me I heard the sound of a horn. Another car was following us at a high speed. I knew its colour before I saw it; it was cream.

I pressed hard on the brake and turned the wheel slightly. I was just able to move in behind the lorry without touching it. The other car passed us and the driver blew his horn wildly. It reached the lorry – and then the lorry turned towards it.

For a moment I thought that the car was going to pass the lorry safely; it was moving very fast. Then the front of the lorry just touched the back of the car. It was only a light touch, but it knocked the car towards the side of the road and the woman at the table.

The driver of that car knew exactly what to do. With the greatest skill he turned it back into the middle of the road. His control was wonderful, much better than mine. He waved angrily at the lorry driver and drove quickly away in a cloud of dust. He was soon out of sight.

We stayed that night in Fontainebleau. A big car was standing outside the hotel, and the back showed signs of damage to the paintwork. It was a cream car, and so I looked for the driver. He was not wearing a red hat or an expensive shirt.

He was a young man from Paris – not like the driver in my dream. He spoke good English, so I asked him if he would like the number of that lorry. I had noticed it, and I was happy to give it to him. But he only laughed; the law won't help you if you pass on the wrong side of the road. To him the whole thing had been a game.

'It tests your skill,' he said. 'If the car is powerful enough, you can do it. But you couldn't do it, not in your car.'

I didn't tell him about my dream, my reason for not passing the lorry. There was no time; he was in a hurry and wanted to reach Paris quickly. It made me think, though. I don't really believe in dreams, of course; but something saved us all from a terrible death.

2.1 Were you right?

1   Look back at your answers to 1.2 on page iv. Then complete these sentences.

In the dream, the driver is in ¹ ...., where people drive on the ² ...., The story-teller is the ³ .... and a ⁴ .... crashes into his car. But, in reality, there is ⁵ .... crash.

2   Which of these are true of the dream (D) and in reality (R)? Tick (✓) them.

		D	R
1	The driver of the cream car is a cheerful man of about forty.		
2	A woman sits outside a white house with a table of flowers.		
3	The lorry turns towards the story-teller's car.		
4	There is another car behind the story-teller.		
5	The lorry turns towards the cream car.		
6	The driver of the cream car is a young man from Paris.		
7	Nobody is hurt.		

2.2 What more did you learn?

Who might say these words in the real events of the story?

Are we going to be in this car much longer?

Can't you pass this lorry? It's making terrible noises.

The flower seller! We're going to die!

B ....

D ....

....

....

Pass me! You can't do it, can you?!

Dad, you nearly killed us all.

A ....

C ....

E ....

....

....

....

2.3 Language in use

Look at the sentence on the right and the example below. Then complete the other sentences with verb forms.

> This **sight**, for some reason, filled me with a terrible fear.

1 This *sight* filled me with fear.   What did you ....*see*............ ?

2 Put your hands on the *controls*.   What do they .... ?

3 Her *death* was unexpected.   When did she .... ?

4 There was an *explosion*.   What .... ?

5 I had a terrible *dream*.   What did you .... ?

6 We've got an *invitation*.   When were you .... ?

7 It is his second *marriage*.   Who has he .... ?

8 His business has been a great *success*.   How did he .... ?

2.4 What's next?

The next story is by D. H. Lawrence, one of Britain's most famous writers. He wrote about human relationships and emotions. This story takes place after World War 1 (1914–18).

Look at the pictures on pages 8–19. How happy do you think the blind man and his wife are, alone on their farm? What are their worries, for themselves and for each other? What effect will the other man, a visitor, have on their lives? Make notes below.

Notes

The Blind Man

D. H. Lawrence

Maurice didn't think much or worry much. While he
had the power of touch, he was happy without sight.

Isabel Pervin was listening for two sounds – for the sound of wheels on the drive outside and for the noise of her husband's footsteps in the hall. It was the late afternoon of a rainy November day. Her dearest and oldest friend was on his way from the station. Her husband, who had been blinded in the war in France, was outside somewhere.

Maurice had been home for a year now. He was badly **scar**red and totally blind, but they had been very happy. Grange Farm was Maurice's own place. The farm workers lived at the back of the house, while Isabel lived with her husband in the comfortable rooms at the front. They had spent most of their time alone together since his return. They talked and sang and read together. She wrote short pieces for a newspaper and he did some work on the farm – simple work, it is true, but it gave him satisfaction. He milked the cows and looked after the pigs and horses. Life was still very full for the blind man, peaceful in darkness. With his wife he had a whole world, rich and real.

But sometimes their happiness left them. In that silent house, Isabel sometimes felt she was going crazy. And sometimes her husband became **despair**ing. She tried then to force the old cheerfulness to continue, but the effort was almost too much for her. At such times she would give anything, anything, to escape.

She looked for a way out. She invited friends. She tried to give her husband some further connection with the outside world. But it was no good. Nobody could understand the depth of the experiences that they had shared in the past year.

But now, in a few weeks' time, her second baby would be born. The first had died while her husband was in France. She looked forward with pleasure to the coming of the second, but she also felt a little anxious. The child would take her love and attention. And then, what about Maurice? What would he do?

It was at this time that Isabel's old friend, Bertie Reid, wrote to her. All her life he had been her friend – like a brother, but better than her own brothers. She loved him, though not in the same way as the man she had chosen to marry.

---

scar /skɑː/ (v/n) to be given a mark on your skin from a deep cut, which never goes away
despair /dɪ'speə/ (v/n) to feel that there is no hope

Bertie was a lawyer, a thoughtful type with a quick mind. Maurice was different. He was slow and sensitive – a big, heavy man. The two men had never been close. Isabel thought they should like each other. But they did not.

So when Maurice was going out to France, she wrote to Bertie saying that she must end her friendship with him.

For nearly two years there had been no communication between the two friends. Then a little note came from Bertie. He wrote of the real pain he felt about Maurice's blindness. Isabel felt a nervous excitement again, and she read the letter to Maurice.

'Ask him to come down,' he said.

'Ask Bertie to come here?'

'Yes – if he wants to.'

Isabel thought about this.

'I know he wants to,' she replied. 'But what about you, Maurice? How would you like it?'

'I should like it.'

'Well – in that case – But I thought you didn't care for him–'

"Oh, I don't know. I might think differently of him now," the blind man replied.

So Bertie was coming, coming this evening, in the November rain and darkness. Isabel looked nervously again at the high windows, where the rain was beating against the glass. Maurice was out in the stable.

She stood up and looked at herself in the mirror. Her face was calm. Her neck made a beautiful line to her shoulder. She had a warm, motherly look.

She passed down the wide hall and put on heavy shoes, a large coat and a man's hat. Then she went outside. It was very dark and very windy. As she walked on, the darkness seemed deeper, and she was sorry she had not brought a lamp. Rain blew against her. She half liked it and she half felt that she did not want to fight against it.

She reached the door of the **stable**. There was no light anywhere. She opened the door and looked in, into total darkness. The sudden smell of horses shocked her. She listened but could only hear the night and the restless movement of a horse.

'Maurice!' she called softly. 'Maurice – are you there?'

stable /'steɪbəl/ (n) a building where horses are kept

Nothing came from the darkness. The rain and the wind were blowing in, so she entered and shut the door. She was conscious of the horses, though she could not see them, and she was afraid.

Then she heard a small noise in the distance. It was Maurice in the other part of the stable. The low sound of his voice as he spoke to the horses came to her in the darkness.

She called quietly, 'Maurice, Maurice – dear!'

'Yes,' he answered. 'Isabel?'

She saw nothing, and the sound of his voice seemed to touch her.

'Won't you come in, dear?' she said.

'Yes, I'm coming. Just half a minute. Bertie hasn't arrived yet, has he?'

'Not yet,' said Isabel.

She wanted him to come to her. When she could not see him, she was frightened of him.

'Bertie won't much enjoy the drive in this weather,' he said, as he closed the door.

'No, he won't!' said Isabel calmly, watching the dark shape at the door. 'Give me your arm, dear.'

Isabel was pleased to be back in the house. She was a little afraid of him out there in the darkness. In the hall he sat down heavily. As he bent down to take off his boots, he didn't seem blind. When he stood up, the blood rushed to his face and neck, and she didn't look at his eyes.

He went away upstairs. She saw him go into the darkness. He did not know that the lamps upstairs were not lit. She heard him in the bathroom.

Maurice moved around almost unconsciously. He seemed to know where things were before he touched them. He didn't think much or worry much. While he had the power of touch, he was happy without sight. It was a pleasure to stretch out his hand and pick up something that he couldn't see, to hold it and own it. He didn't try to remember what it looked like. He didn't want to. This new consciousness had become natural to him. He was generally happy and he had a burning love for Isabel. But at times despair swept over him and destroyed his happiness. Then he suffered.

But tonight he was still calm, though his senses were a little sharp. His hearing was too sharp. He was conscious of all the sounds in the house. As he went to his room he heard a vehicle arrive.

Then came Isabel's voice, like a bell ringing. 'Is it you, Bertie?'

And a man's voice answered out of the wind. 'Hello, Isabel. There you are. You're looking as fit as ever.'

'Oh yes,' said Isabel. 'I'm very well. How are you? Rather thin, I think–'

'Worked to death. But I'm all right. How's Maurice? Isn't he here?'

'Oh yes, he's upstairs, changing his clothes. Yes, he's well.'

They moved away. Maurice heard no more. But a childish sense of despair had come over him. He felt shut out – like a child in the company of adults. He dressed himself and went downstairs.

Isabel was alone in the sitting room. She watched him enter.

'Did you hear Bertie come, Maurice?' she said.

'Yes – isn't he here?'

'He's in his room. He looks very thin and tired.'

Bertie came down. He was a little dark man, with a very big forehead, thin hair, and sad, large eyes. He had strange, short legs. Isabel watched him pause at the door, and look nervously at her husband.

Bertie went across to Maurice.

The blind man put his hand out and Bertie took it. Isabel watched them anxiously, and then looked away again.

'Come,' she said. 'Come to the table. Aren't you both hungry?'

They sat down.

Maurice felt for his place, his knife and fork. Bertie picked up a little bowl of flowers from the table, and held them to his nose.

'They have a lovely sweet smell,' he said. 'Where do they come from?'

'From the garden – under the windows. Bertie, do you remember the flowers under Aunt Bell's wall?'

The two friends looked at each other and smiled.

The meal continued and Isabel and Bertie spoke easily together. The blind man was silent. He ate carefully but quickly. He could never accept any help.

After the meal, the three sat around the fire. Isabel put more wood on and Bertie noticed a slight slowness in her movements.

'Will you be pleased when the child comes, Isabel?' he said.

She looked at him with a smile.

'Yes, I shall be very pleased. So will you, Maurice, won't you?' she added.

'Yes, I shall,' replied her husband.

'We are both looking forward to it so much,' she said.

'Yes, of course,' said Bertie.

He was three or four years older than Isabel and had never married. He had other women friends – but they were friends, not lovers. If they seemed to come too close, he pulled away. Isabel knew him very well, his kindness, but also his weakness, which made him unable ever to enter into any close human relationships. He was ashamed of himself because he couldn't marry. He wanted

14

to, but he couldn't. Deep down inside he was afraid. He became a successful lawyer, a rich man and a great social success. But at the centre he felt that he was nothing.

Isabel looked at his sad face and his short little legs. She looked at his dark grey eyes. There was something childlike in him and she loved him. At the same time she pitied and disliked his weakness. He understood this.

Suddenly, Bertie spoke to Maurice.

'Isabel tells me that you have not suffered too badly from losing your sight.'

Maurice straightened himself.

'No,' he said, 'not too badly. You stop worrying about many things.'

'And that is good,' said Bertie. 'But what is it that takes the place of worry?'

Maurice was slow in replying.

'There is something,' Maurice said. 'But I couldn't tell you what it is.'

Then the blind man was silent. He stood up slowly, a big, uncomfortable figure. He wanted to go away.

'Do you mind,' he said, 'if I go and speak to the farm manager? I won't be long.'

'No – go along, dear,' said Isabel.

And he went out. A silence came over the two friends. The wind blew loudly outside. Rain beat like a drum on the windows. The wood in the fireplace burned slowly with hot small flames. Bertie seemed uncomfortable. There were dark circles around his eyes. Isabel looked into the fire.

'The child coming seems to make me calm. I feel there's nothing to worry about,' she said.

'A good thing, I should say,' Bertie replied slowly.

'If I didn't feel anxious about Maurice, I'd be quite happy.'

The evening passed slowly. Isabel looked at the clock.

'It's nearly ten o'clock,' she said. 'Where can Maurice be?'

Bertie looked at her. 'Would you like me to go out and see?'

'Well – if you wouldn't mind. I'd go, but–' She did not want to make the effort.

Bertie put on an old coat and took a lamp. He left by the side door. He felt nervous and strangely empty. He walked slowly through the wet and stormy night.

At last he opened the door of a stable and, looking in, he saw Maurice standing, listening.

'Who is that?' said Maurice.

'It's me,' said Bertie. He entered and shut the door behind him.

'You came to look for me?' he asked.

'Isabel was a little worried,' said Bertie.

'I'll come in.'

'I hope I'm not in your way at all,' said Bertie, rather shyly.

'My way?' Maurice said. 'Not a bit. I'm pleased Isabel has someone to talk to. I'm afraid that I am in the way. I know I'm not very good company. Is Isabel all right, do you think? She's not unhappy, is she?'

'I don't think so.'

'What does she say?'

'She says she's very happy – only a little worried about you,' said Bertie carefully.

'She needn't worry about me. I'm afraid that she'll find me dull, always alone with me down here.'

Maurice lowered his voice and took a deep breath. 'Bertie,' he asked, 'is my face a very ugly sight? Do you mind telling me?'

'There is a scar,' said Bertie, surprised. 'But one feels pity more than shock at the sight of it.'

'A bad scar, though,' said Maurice.

'Oh, yes.'

There was a pause.

'I don't really know you, do I?' Maurice said suddenly in a strange voice.

'Probably not,' said Bertie.

'Do you mind if I touch you?'

Bertie stepped back but said, in a small voice, 'Not at all.'

He suffered as the blind man stretched out a strong hand and felt his head. He covered the face of the smaller man, touching the forehead, the closed eyes, the small nose, the mouth, the strong chin.

'You seem young,' Maurice said quietly, at last.

Bertie stood, nearly destroyed, unable to answer.

'Your head seems soft,' Maurice continued. 'So do your hands. Touch my eyes, will you? Touch my scar.'

Bertie was sickened by the idea, but he was under the power of the blind man. He lifted his hand, and touched the scar. Maurice suddenly covered it with his own hand, pressed the fingers of the other man onto his scarred eyes. He stayed in this position for a minute or more while Bertie froze, helpless.

Then, suddenly, Maurice took the other man's hand away and stood holding it in his own.

'Oh my God,' he said. 'We shall know each other now, shan't we? We shall know each other now.'

Bertie could not answer. He looked at the blind man silently and in terror, despairing at his own weakness. He knew that he could not answer. He had an unreasonable fear that the other man would suddenly destroy him. Maurice was actually filled with a burning desire for friendship – and Bertie only wanted to escape.

'It's all right now, as long as we live. We're all right together now, aren't we?' Maurice said.

'Yes,' said Bertie.

Maurice turned to pick up his coat.

'Come,' he said, 'we'll go to Isabel.'

Bertie took the lamp and opened the door. The two men went in silence.

Isabel heard their footsteps and looked up anxiously as they entered. There seemed a strange happiness in Maurice. Bertie looked tired. His eyes were darker than before.

'What is it?' she asked.

'We've become friends,' said Maurice.

She looked at Bertie. He met her eyes with a despairing look.

'I'm so pleased,' she said, confused.

'Yes,' said Maurice.

Isabel took his hand with both of hers and held it tight.

'You'll be happier now, dear,' she said.

But she was watching Bertie. She knew that he had one desire – to escape from this friendship which had been forced on him. He could not accept that he had been touched by the blind man.

Activities 3

3.1 Were you right?

Look back at your answers to Activity 2.4. Then answer this question: Which of these experiences have Maurice and Isabel shared in the last year?

1 ☐ They have lost their first child.

2 ☐ Isabel has felt that she is going mad.

3 ☐ Isabel is expecting a second child.

4 ☐ They have lived at Grange Farm.

5 ☐ Maurice has felt despair.

6 ☐ Maurice has gone blind.

7 ☐ They have been happy.

3.2 What else did you learn?

1 How do these people feel towards each other at the end of the story? Write these words in the boxes.

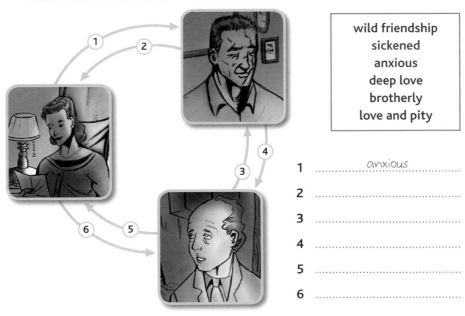

wild friendship
sickened
anxious
deep love
brotherly
love and pity

1 .... *anxious* ....

2 ....

3 ....

4 ....

5 ....

6 ....

2 Work with another student. You are two of the farm workers at Grange Farm. You live at the back of the house. Talk about Maurice and Isabel. What do you think about their lives? Will they be happy?

3.3 Language in use

Look at the sentence on the right. Then make these sentences into one in the same way. Use *who*, *whose* and *which*.

> Her husband, **who had been blinded in the war in France**, was outside somewhere.

1 Isabel was waiting for Bertie. Bertie was late.
   Isabel was waiting for Bertie, who was late.

2 Maurice went upstairs. Maurice didn't know that the lights were off.
   ....
   ....

3 Bertie finally arrived. Bertie was like a brother to Isabel.
   ....
   ....

4 The stable door blew in the wind. The door was open.
   ....
   ....

5 Bertie looked at the scar. The scar was long and red.
   ....
   ....

6 Isabel looked at Bertie. Bertie's eyes showed his despair.
   ....
   ....

3.4 What's next?

1 **Read the first part of the next story, to the middle of page 22. Then discuss these questions and make notes.**

   a Which adjectives in these lines describe Mr Beaseley's life?
   ....

   b What would he do if he suddenly had a lot of money?
   ....

2 **What would you do if you suddenly had a lot of money? Tell the class. Who has the most interesting idea?**

It Happened Near a Lake

John Collier

Mrs Beaseley went with him. She hated it; but she was prepared to do anything that reduced her husband's pleasure.

M r Beaseley was fifty. As he washed, he examined his face in the mirror. 'I'm older,' he thought. 'But what do I care? I don't care, even if Maria does. And she's getting old, too!'

He finished dressing and hurried downstairs. He thought anxiously that he was probably late for breakfast. Immediately after breakfast he had to open his shop, and that always kept him busy until ten o'clock at night. He never made much money, although he worked so hard. Sometimes, during the day, Maria Beaseley came into the shop and explained the mistakes that he was making. She did this even when there were customers there.

He found a little happiness every morning when he opened the newspaper. While he was reading it, he could escape from his dull life. For a short time he could forget. On Fridays he enjoyed himself more than on other days. On Fridays he received his copy of a magazine called *Scientific Discoveries*. With *Scientific Discoveries* he escaped from the dull house and his hopeless life into a more exciting world.

◆

On this particular morning, good news came to Mr Beaseley in his own home. It came in a long envelope from a lawyer.

'Believe it or not, my dear,' Mr Beaseley said to his wife. 'Someone has died and left me four hundred thousand dollars.'

'What?' she said. 'Where? Let me see! Don't keep the letter to yourself like that! Give it to me!'

'Go on!' he said. 'Read it! Push your nose into it! Do you think it will help you?'

'Oh!' she cried. 'The money has already made you unpleasant!'

'Yes,' he said thoughtfully. 'I've been left four hundred thousand dollars. Four hundred thousand!'

'We'll be able to have a flat in New York,' she said, 'or a little house in Miami.'

'You can have half the money,' said Mr Beaseley. 'You can do what you like with it. But I intend to travel.'

Mrs Beaseley heard these words without pleasure. He belonged to her. She never liked losing anything that belonged to her. She always wanted to keep everything, even things that had become old and useless.

'So you want to leave me!' she cried.

'I want to see other places, unusual places, different places. In *Scientific Discoveries* it says that there are people with very long necks. I want to see them. And I want to see the very small people who live in Africa, and some of the strange animals and birds. I want to visit the old cities of the Yucatán in Mexico. I have offered you half the money because you like city life. You like mixing with the rich and the famous, but I prefer to travel. If you want to come with me, come.'

She did not have to think long before answering. 'I will come,' she said. 'And don't forget that I'm doing it for you. When you're tired of walking around with your mouth open, we'll buy a house. We'll have a flat in New York and a house in Miami.'

So Mrs Beaseley went with him. She hated it; but she was prepared to do anything that reduced her husband's pleasure. Their journeys took them into deep forests. Their bedroom walls and floors were often made of plain wood; but outside the window there were beautiful views. The colours of the flowers and the straightness of the trees looked fine in the bright light.

In the high mountains of the Andes their window was a square of burning blue. Sometimes a small white cloud appeared in a lower corner of the square. On islands in the sun they stayed in huts by the sea. There the sea brought offerings of plants and sea **creatures** to their door in the mornings. Mr Beaseley was glad, but his wife preferred bottles of wine. She dreamed every day of a flat in New York; or she thought about the little house in Miami. She tried endlessly to punish the man who kept her from them.

If a beautiful bird came to rest on a branch over her husband's head, she gave a terrible cry. Then the bird flew away before Mr Beaseley had the time to examine it. When they planned a trip to the Yucatán, she told him the wrong time for the start of the journey. Often, while he was trying to watch an interesting animal, she told him that she had something in her eye. So he had to look into it and get the thing out. Usually he found nothing.

She wanted to stay in Buenos Aires for a long time. She had to have her hair done; she also needed some better clothes. Mr Beaseley agreed to these trips because he wanted to be fair to her.

They took rooms in a comfortable hotel. One day, when his wife was out shopping, Mr Beaseley met a little Portuguese doctor. Soon they were talking happily together. They discussed some of the animals that lived in South America.

creature /ˈkriːtʃə/ (n) an animal, fish or insect

23

'I have recently returned from the River Amazon,' said the doctor. 'In one of the lakes there is a very strange creature. It is unknown to science, but the Indians have seen it. It is very big. It lives in the water and has a very long neck. Its teeth are like knives.'

Mr Beaseley was terribly excited. 'What a **monster**!' he cried happily.

'Yes,' said the Portuguese doctor. 'It is certainly interesting.'

'I must go there!' cried Mr Beaseley. 'I must talk to those Indians. If there's a monster in the lake, I must see it. Will you show me the way? Can you come with me?'

The doctor agreed, and they decided to prepare for the trip immediately. Mrs Beaseley returned from the shops and learned of the new plan with little pleasure. The two men explained that they would live near the unknown lake. They would spend their time with the Indians.

She was not pleased, and she spoke rudely to the little doctor. He just replied politely. He had no need to worry. He was going to be paid well for his help.

Mrs Beaseley complained loudly all the way up the river. She told her husband that there was no monster in the lake. She said that the doctor was lying to him. Although this was the way she always spoke, her husband was hurt. He felt ashamed in front of the Portuguese man. His wife's voice was also very loud and sharp, so every animal hurried away from them. Mr Beaseley saw nothing of the animals except their back legs. They all left the great river and the terrible voice at high speed and hid themselves in the dark forest behind the biggest trees.

The little party reached the lake after many days on the river.

'How do we know that this is the right place?' Mrs Beaseley said to her husband. She was watching the doctor, who was talking to some Indians. 'It is probably just a lake. It's not a special one. What are those Indians saying to him? You can't understand a word. You're ready to believe anything, aren't you? You'll never see the monster. Only a stupid person would believe that story.'

Mr Beaseley did not reply. The doctor continued his conversation with the Indians, and they gave him some useful information. They told him about an empty grass hut which was near the lake. The little party found this hut with great difficulty, and they stayed in it for several days. Mr Beaseley watched the lake every day, but he never saw the monster. In fact, he saw nothing at all. Mrs Beaseley was very satisfied with the result of their long journey, but she continued to look angry.

One day she shouted at her husband. 'I will not live this kind of life any longer,' she said. 'I've followed you from one place to another. I've tried to watch you and take care of you all the time. I've travelled hundreds of kilometres in an

monster /ˈmɒnstə/ (n) a very large, ugly, frightening animal

open boat with Indians. Now you're throwing your money away on a man who only wants to rob you. We shall leave for Parà in the morning.'

'You can go if you wish,' he said. 'I'll write you a cheque for two hundred thousand dollars. Perhaps you can ask an Indian to take you down the river in a boat. But I will not come with you.'

'We shall see,' she said. She had no wish to leave her husband alone. She was afraid that he might enjoy himself.

He wrote out the cheque and gave it to her. She still continued to talk about leaving him, but she stayed.

She got up early the next morning and went outside the hut. She decided to have breakfast alone, and walked angrily towards some trees intending to pick some fruit. But she had not gone far before she noticed a mark on the sand. It was a very large footprint nearly a metre wide. The toes seemed to have sharp points, and the next footprint was three metres away.

Mrs Beaseley looked without interest at the marks which the monster had left. Her only feeling was anger at the thought of her husband's success. She was angry because the Portuguese doctor had been right. She did not cry out in excitement; she did not call to the sleeping men. She only gave a kind of bitter laugh.

Then she picked up a small branch which was lying on the ground. The monster's footprints had never been seen before by a European, but she brushed the first one with the branch until it disappeared. When she had finished, she smiled to herself. There was now no sign of the footprint, and so she looked for the next one. She cleaned that away, too. Further on she saw another, and then one more. She brushed earth over them. Then she saw another, moved towards it, and made it disappear. She continued in this way, holding the branch with both hands. Soon every footprint down to the edge of the lake had gone. The last footprint was partly in the water. The monster had clearly gone back to the lake.

Mrs Beaseley stood up straight. She looked coldly back towards the hut.

'I will tell you about this,' she said to herself, thinking of her sleeping husband, 'when we are far away. We shall be in our house in Miami, and you will be an old man. You will never see the footprint or the monster. You'll be too old to do anything then.'

At that moment there was a sound in the water behind her and large teeth closed on her. The Portuguese doctor had described these teeth very well: they were exactly like knives. He had described a number of other details, but she had no time to see if they were correct. After she had given one short cry, she was pulled under the water. Her cry was not heard by either of the men. She had used her voice too much during the past weeks, and it was tired.

A short time later Mr Beaseley awoke and saw that his wife was absent. He went to talk to the doctor, and asked him if he had seen her. The doctor, of course, knew nothing and went back to sleep. Mr Beaseley went outside and looked around for his wife, but he could see nothing. He returned to his friend.

'I think my wife has run away,' he explained. 'I've found her footprints. They lead down to the lake. I expect she saw an Indian in his boat who has taken her away from here. She was talking about leaving yesterday. She wants to find a small house in Miami.'

'That is not a bad place,' the doctor replied. 'But Buenos Aires is probably a better one. I'm sorry we haven't found the monster, my dear friend. Let us go back to Buenos Aires. I will show you some things there that will surprise you. They are very different from anything here, of course.'

'You're a very good friend,' said Mr Beaseley. 'You make even life in a city seem attractive.'

'If you get tired of it,' the Portuguese said, 'we can always move on. I know some wonderful islands, with friendly people on them. We can visit them after we leave the cities.'

4.1 Were you right?

Look back at your answers to Activity 3.4. Then decide if these sentences are true (✓) or false (✗).

1 ☐ Mr and Mrs Beaseley love each other very much.
2 ☐ She wants to leave him.
3 ☐ They travel to South America.
4 ☐ The lake is near the Amazon.
5 ☐ There is a monster in the lake.
6 ☐ Mrs Beaseley leaves her husband.
7 ☐ Mr Beaseley goes home.

4.2 What more did you learn?

1 Tick (✓) the places that the Beaseleys definitely visit.

☐ Africa   ☐ Buenos Aires   ☐ Miami
☐ New York   ☐ Parà   ☐ Portugal
☐ the Andes   ☐ the River Amazon   ☐ the Yucatán

2 Discuss in pairs why these are important in the story.

A

B

C

D

.3 Language in use

Look at the sentence on the right. Then report these words from the story.

> She told him **that she had** something in **her** eye.

1 'You can have half the money,' said Mr Beaseley.
   Mrs Beaseley told his wife that ...she could have half the money.

2 'I will come,' she said.
   Mrs Beaseley said that ....
   ....

3 'I have recently returned from the River Amazon,' said the doctor.
   The doctor told them that ....
   ....

4 'If there's a monster in the lake, I must see it,' cried Mr Beaseley.
   Mr Beaseley said that ....
   ....

5 'You're throwing money away on a man who only wants to rob you.'
   Mrs Beaseley told her husband that ....
   ....

6 'I think my wife has run away.'
   Mr Beaseley said that ....
   ....

.4 What's next?

Read this statement from the next story and discuss the questions below it. Then write answers to the questions. Write notes.

'When you give a man something for nothing, he is never grateful. He turns against you.'

1 Why do people give away money, clothes and other things that they own?
2 How do they feel when they give them?
3 How does it feel to receive them?
4 How true is the statement above?

Notes

The Ugly American
and the Ugly Sarkhanese

W. J. Lederer and E. Burdick

Sarkhanese men, he said, must not handle machines. They had never done that before, and they must not do it now.

Homer Atkins, an ugly man, looked angrily round the room. The other men sat there in their beautiful clothes and returned his look coldly. He was the only one without a tie, and the only engineer. One of the others was the **ambassador**. Atkins wanted to tell them all that they were stupid; but it is not easy to tell an ambassador that he is stupid. The others, too, were important to their different governments. So he did not say it.

'I was asked to come here, gentlemen,' he said, 'to give advice. I build roads and move earth. That's my job. You say that you want roads. I can tell you, though, that you don't need any. I've been here for ten months, and I've walked all over the country. I've talked to a thousand people, and I've sent in my report.'

'But Mr Atkins,' said one of the well-dressed gentlemen, 'you haven't told us much about the roads. Where should they go?'

'You don't need any. You need things that the people here can make: small things, but useful things. What do the people care about roads for the army? Here you can think of nothing else: roads, only roads. But go out into the country, and take a look. You've got some good people out there. Build some factories for them. Let them make cans and put food in them. Forget the roads until you've got more money.'

'Mr Atkins, this is not your business. We asked you where the roads should go. No one has asked you if you prefer roads or factories. You must leave that sort of decision to others. They must decide, not you.'

'Who should decide? People like you? Which of you has been out into the country? What do you know about the villages?'

There was a silence.

'Which of you has been out into the country?' Atkins asked again. The silence was unbroken. There were many red faces in the room.

'Build a factory to make bricks,' Atkins said. 'Let some of the people take stone out of the ground too. There's a lot of very fine stone out there which they

---

ambassador /æmˈbæsədə/ (n) an important official who acts for his or her country in a foreign capital

can use for building. And make use of that good earth near the coast to plant things.'

'That's the work of others,' someone said. 'You know nothing about the land. You're a road builder.'

'Very well!' Atkins said. He got up and walked out of the room; but the ambassador followed him.

'Come and have a drink,' the ambassador said. 'I like the things that you say.'

'No one else likes them,' said Atkins with a bitter laugh.

'Mr Atkins,' the ambassador said, 'are you willing to go to Sarkhan?'

'Why? Have you any problems there?'

They were sitting together with their drinks. 'Sarkhan is a country with a lot of hills,' the ambassador said. 'Food is grown on **terraces** on the hills. People have to work hard to bring water up from the rivers below. The fields above need the water, but it is slow work. Can you help us with that problem? Can you find an easy way of bringing water to the terraces?'

terrace /'terəs/ (n) a flat piece of ground which has been cut out of a hill

'Perhaps! Perhaps!' Atkins took a pencil and began to draw. 'You need a simple **pump**,' he said. He was busy for fifteen minutes and did not speak. 'Well, it may be interesting,' he said then. 'Yes, it may be quite interesting.'

Two weeks later Atkins and his wife, who was almost as ugly as her husband, flew to Sarkhan. They went to live in a small house near Haidho.

The house had earth floors, and there was little water. There were thousands of insects, and one Sarkhanese boy. Ong was nine, and had dark eyes. He appeared at exactly six o'clock every morning and stayed all day.

Emma Atkins enjoyed herself in Sarkhan. She liked housework and she kept her house looking nice. It was as clean and attractive as the houses of her neighbours.

Homer Atkins was busy with his pump. It was a water pump that villagers would work by hand. The idea developed very slowly in his mind. People needed good pumps to lift water, but carrying it up was hard and slow. One man carried it to the terrace, and another man emptied it there. The Sarkhanese had been doing this for many years, and they did not like the thought of change. There seemed to be no reason for change; but Atkins knew that he must find a better way of moving the water. Talking was useless. He had to do something to help.

A simple pump needed three things. First, it had to have cheap pipes. This was not a difficult problem to solve. He had decided that the pipes could be made of **bamboo**. There was a lot of bamboo in the place. Second, he had to make the pump itself, and he found a solution to this too. Outside many Sarkhanese villages there were old lorries which the army no longer wanted. Atkins had taken a number of parts from one of these and put them together. With these he could lift the water nine metres.

The third problem had not been solved. He needed something to drive the pump.

He talked to his wife about this problem. 'It must be something that is found here in Sarkhan,' he explained. 'I don't want to bring something from abroad. If I do that, it will cost too much; and the Sarkhanese might not understand it. Most of the farmers haven't been abroad.'

'Why don't you give these nice people some good engines?' Emma asked. 'You've got all that money in the bank in Pittsburg. You're rich enough.'

'You know the reason,' he said. 'When you give a man something for nothing, he is never grateful. He turns against you. If this pump is going to work well, it must be a Sarkhanese pump. If I gave them part of it, it would be my pump.'

---

pump /pʌmp/ (n) a machine which forces liquid or gas into or out of something
bamboo /ˌbæmˈbuː/ (n) a tall, hollow plant, used to make furniture

Emma smiled at Homer. She turned and looked out of the window. She saw a group of Sarkhanese on bicycles; they were riding, as usual, towards the markets of Haidho. She watched them for a few moments. Then she turned round suddenly, and her eyes showed her excitement.

'Why don't you use bicycles?' she asked. 'There are millions of them in this country, and people must throw them away sometimes. Couldn't you use old bicycle parts to drive each pump?'

Atkins looked at Emma's face and slowly sat up straight.

'I believe you've found the answer, old girl,' he said softly. 'Yes! We can do it.' He began to walk round the room. Emma, with a little smile, returned to her cooking. In a few moments she heard the sound of papers; she knew that her Homer was drawing something. Two hours later he was still drawing. An hour after that he started to drink beer. When the time came for dinner, he had drunk a lot of beer: about six bottles.

'I think I've found the answer,' he said. He began to explain the machine to her. She made him sit down and eat his dinner; but he ate very fast and talked about his drawings all the time. Emma watched her husband fondly. She was proud of him. She was happy when he was happy. Today she was filled with happiness.

'Stop drinking beer, Homer,' she said. 'And don't forget that it was my idea about the bicycle.'

'Your idea?' he shouted. 'Woman, you're crazy! It's been at the back of my mind all the time. You just made me remember it.'

Two days later he had all the designs for a working machine. Every part of it could be found in the country; nothing needed to come from anywhere else. There were probably enough old bicycles to make 2,000 pumps; but first he had to make two pumps that worked well. At this time Emma gave him another piece of good advice.

'Now, listen, Homer,' she said. 'You've got a good machine there, and I'm proud of you. But the Sarkhanese won't use it immediately just because it's good. Go slowly. Let them use the machine themselves, and in their own way. If you try to force them, they'll never use it.'

'Well, tell me what to do,' Atkins said. He knew she was right, and he was grateful to her.

Emma calmly explained her plan to Homer. He realized that she had been thinking of this for some time. It was a beautiful plan. He wished that some of the government men could hear it. He started to use the plan the next day.

He drove to the small village of Chang Dong. The village was built on a steep hill, a four-hour drive from Haidho, where a hundred people lived in fifteen or twenty houses. The earth was rich, but it was a poor village. The terraces were so high above the river that carrying the water up there took a long time. The men were always tired in Chang Dong.

Atkins politely asked where the home of the headman was. He talked to the headman in his own language. This pleased the headman, and during their discussion he helped Atkins to find the right words.

Atkins told the headman that he was an American engineer who had designed a new kind of pump. This could lift water to the terraces, and he wanted to

develop it. He did not try to explain it in detail, since the headman was not an engineer. He said that he wanted to make and sell pumps. He wanted the headman to find a clever Sarkhanese who knew something about machines. Atkins said that he would pay well for this man's time and skill. The man would also share any money that they made from the business.

The old man understood clearly, and they began to discuss the new mechanic's pay. Both the headman and Atkins were soon satisfied. They shook hands, and the headman went off to find the mechanic.

He returned with a small man known as Jeepo. Atkins did not listen very closely to the headman's words. He was studying the mechanic, and he liked the look of the man.

Jeepo looked very strong, and his hands were as dirty as Atkins's own hands. It was clear that in the world of engines they would work well together. Jeepo was also as ugly as Atkins. The two men smiled at one another.

'The headman says that you're a good mechanic,' Atkins said. 'I understand that you normally repair lorries. Have you ever worked on anything else?'

Jeepo smiled. 'I've worked on pumps, cars, bicycles and a few planes.'

'Did you always understand everything that you did?'

'Does anyone understand everything?' Jeepo asked. 'I think I can work on any machine. But that's only my own opinion. Try me.'

'We'll start this afternoon,' Atkins said. 'There are a lot of things in my car outside. We'll take them out and start immediately.'

By the middle of the afternoon they had done a lot. Six metres of bamboo pipe had been fixed together. The bottom of the pipe was put into the river near the village. The top part of the pipe was fixed to the pump which Atkins had designed. An old bicycle was placed above the pump. Both of its wheels had been taken off. Jeepo had put these things together himself, without Atkins's help. Everything was ready in the late afternoon.

Atkins drank some beer, and waited calmly. The headman and two or three others were sitting beside him. He could feel that they were very excited. They understood the purpose of the machine, but they did not believe that it would work.

'Sir, the machine is ready,' Jeepo said quietly. 'I'm ready to start the bicycle. Then we can see if it works.'

Atkins agreed. Jeepo climbed on the bicycle and began to cycle. The pump worked slowly. Jeepo cycled faster, and the pipes made strange noises. For several seconds there was no other sound. Then suddenly some dirty brown water rushed out of the top of the pipe. Jeepo did not stop or smile; but the headman and the others were very excited.

'This is a clever machine,' the headman said to Atkins. 'In a few minutes you have lifted a lot of water. It is more than we can lift in five hours.'

Atkins did not reply. He was waiting for Jeepo. He had a feeling that Jeepo was not completely satisfied.

Jeepo continued to cycle, and looked down at the machine. He saw that some changes were needed. He called out to Atkins to tell him about them. When the small field was covered with water, he got off the bicycle.

'It's a very clever machine, Mr Atkins,' Jeepo said. 'But it is not a machine for this country.'

Atkins looked at him carefully. 'Why not?' he asked.

Jeepo did not reply immediately. He moved silently round the machine; then he stopped and faced Atkins.

'The machine works well,' he said. 'But a man who wants one must have a second bicycle. In this country, Mr Atkins, very few people have two bicycles. They haven't enough money. If you cannot find another way to drive the pump, your clever machine is useless.'

For a moment Atkins felt angry. But he stayed calm when he remembered Emma's advice.

'What happens to all the old bicycles in this country?' he asked Jeepo. 'Aren't there enough of them to drive the pumps?'

'There are no old bicycles in this country,' Jeepo said. 'We ride bicycles until they fall to pieces. When a man throws his bicycle away, it's too old for anything else.'

'So what would you do, Jeepo?' Atkins asked. 'You understand machines. You should have some ideas.'

For a time Jeepo gave no answer. He sat in the field and looked at the strange machine. He said nothing for ten minutes. Then he stood up and walked slowly to the machine. He started it again. Then he walked back to his place in the field.

Atkins went over to Jeepo and sat down beside him. For fifteen minutes the two men sat quietly, studying the machine. Atkins spoke first.

'Perhaps we could make a wooden **frame**,' he said.

'The frame's cheap enough,' Jeepo answered. 'It's the other parts that cost the money.'

For ten more minutes they sat together. The headman and the others were talking all the time, but Atkins said nothing. He and Jeepo thought of a number of different solutions to their problem, but each one was useless.

frame /freɪm/ (n) the main support that a machine is built around

When darkness was falling, Jeepo suddenly stood up. He walked to the bicycle, and began to cycle hard. Water rushed out of the top of the pipe. He shouted ideas at Atkins.

He suggested making another frame from bamboo. This frame could then hold an ordinary bicycle; the back wheel of the bicycle could drive the pump. They would have to change the machine slightly. After that, everything would be easy. Each family had a bicycle for use on the roads. They could use that same bicycle to drive the pump.

Atkins showed his pleasure. 'This man has made a great discovery,' he told the headman. 'People can use a bicycle on the roads and also for the pump. Jeepo's idea has made everything possible. He must get half of the money that will come out of this business.'

The headman spoke a few words to the other men; then he turned to Atkins. 'Are you suggesting that you and Jeepo should build pumps together?' he asked.

'Yes. I want to enter into business with Jeepo. We'll start a factory and build this kind of pump. We'll sell the pumps to anyone who'll buy them. They will not need to pay the whole price immediately; they can pay over three years. Jeepo will have to work hard, as hard as I do myself.'

The old men did not seem sure that Atkins would work hard. There was a lot of argument, but Jeepo himself said nothing. He stood by the machine and touched it. Then he left it. He spoke to the headman.

'I've listened to all of you, and I've said nothing,' he said. 'You're all silly old men. This American is good with his hands. He built this machine with them. You people do not understand machines; but Mr Atkins and I understand each other. I will enter into business with him if he's ready to accept me.'

The headman looked quite ashamed. 'Jeepo's quite right,' he said. 'We can believe in this American.'

'When we've made some pumps,' Atkins said, 'we'll write about them. We'll send the information to every part of the country. The village of Chang Dong will become famous.'

Two days later Jeepo and Atkins rented a building just outside the village. They hired twelve men to do the work. They bought the necessary equipment and materials, and in a week the work was going well. A small sign was put up over the door: The Jeepo-Atkins Company Limited. Jeepo and Atkins worked eighteen or twenty hours a day. They taught other men and tested materials. They worked hard and became angry. They used bad language and shouted a lot.

Emma Atkins moved from Haidho to the village of Chang Dong. She bought food in the village and cooked it at home. She took food to the factory and the other women of the village did the same.

Once an important man came to the factory and spoke seriously to Atkins. Sarkhanese men, he said, must not handle machines. They had never done that before, and they must not do it now.

Atkins said exactly what he thought. The visitor drove away with a red face and an angry expression. Atkins went happily back to his work.

At the end of six weeks they had built twenty-three pumps. When the twenty-fourth pump was ready, Atkins called the men together. Jeepo faced them with him.

'We are now coming to the difficult part of this business,' Jeepo said. 'You have worked well to make these pumps, but now you have to sell them. Each of you must take two pumps and go out to get orders. Show the two pumps that you have. When you sell one, we'll give you a tenth of its price.'

The men liked this plan very much. It was new to them, but they were quite ready to try it. The next morning twelve **cart**s stood outside the factory. Two pumps were lifted onto each cart, and each cart travelled out to a different part of the country.

Now the villagers could only wait. They knew that they must get some orders for pumps. The factory was useless without orders. The factory was now very important to the people of Chang Dong, and they did not want it to close.

Four days passed, but none of the men returned. Then, on the fifth morning, one of the men arrived back.

He was driving his cart at high speed, which is difficult. The animal that was pulling it almost fell. Dust flew through the air as the wheels turned. Everyone in the village rushed to the factory, to hear the news. The cart was covered with dust. It was empty.

The driver climbed slowly down from his seat. He was important, and he knew it. He walked calmly towards Jeepo and Atkins, and stood there in front of them.

cart /kɑːt/ (n) a vehicle that is pulled by hand or by animals

'I wish to inform you, sirs, that I have not followed your instructions,' he said. A slow smile spread over his face. 'You told me to bring back the two pumps, but I could not do that. I have received orders for eight pumps, but two of the men wanted their pumps immediately. They needed water badly; their plants were almost dead. I did not want to give them the pumps, but I had to. I hope that I have not made a bad mistake!'

Everyone in the crowd turned and looked at Jeepo and Atkins. Those two men, covered in dirt from their work, looked at each other for a moment. Then suddenly they shouted with happiness. The whole crowd began to shout with joy. The villagers were filled with happiness. They held a party, and the whole village went to it.

The next morning everyone got up early. The first to arrive at the factory were Jeepo and Atkins. Soon the village rang with the sound of work. People went to the factory and looked in. Jeepo and Atkins were in the middle of a violent argument; they were discussing changes to the design of the pump. Emma Atkins was spreading out a large breakfast in front of the two men, but they were taking no notice of the food.

The argument continued loudly.

5.1 Were you right?

Look back at your answers to Activity 4.4. Then decide which of these pieces of advice Homer would give to someone starting a new business in Sarkhan. Write ✓ or ✗ .

1 ☐ Your idea must be cheap to make.
2 ☐ Use only materials that you can find in Sarkhan.
3 ☐ Pay for as much as you can yourself.
4 ☐ Bring in parts from abroad.
5 ☐ Let the Sarkhanese accept the idea slowly.
6 ☐ Involve local people in making the product.
7 ☐ Share the money that you make with people who work for it.
8 ☐ Pay the local people as little as you can.
9 ☐ Give the product free to people who need it.

5.2 What more did you learn?

Write the correct words for the parts of the Chang Dong Pump in the boxes.

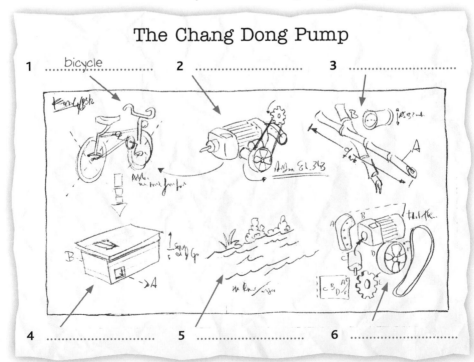

The Chang Dong Pump

1 bicycle
2 ....
3 ....

4 ....
5 ....
6 ....

.3 Language in use

Look at the sentences on the right. Then complete the sentences below which describe the invention before its final stage, with the correct passive verb form.

> The bottom of the pipe **was put** into the river near the village. Six metres of bamboo pipe **had been fixed** together.

First, the top part of the pipe [1] .... *was fixed* .... (fix) to the pump. An old bicycle [2] .... (place) above the pump. The bicycle wheels [3] .... (already take off). Then the water [4] .... (pump) up from the river by twelve men who [5] .... (hire) by Homer and Jeepo. By the end of the six weeks, twenty-three pumps [6] .... (make).

.4 What's next?

Read these lines from the next story, *Hilary's Aunt*. Then discuss possible answers to the questions and make notes. Was it kind to want his aunt to live any longer? Would it not be better for her to die now?

1 Why might it be better for the aunt if she died?
2 Why might it be better for her nephew?
3 How might he help her to die?

Notes

Hilary's Aunt

Cyril Hare

Was it kind to want his aunt to live any longer? Would it not be better for her to die now?

Hilary Smith belonged to a good family, and his father never failed to let people know this fact. Old Mr Smith was a man whose ideas and behaviour belonged to the traditions of nineteenth-century gentlemen.

Unfortunately, Hilary himself had some trouble with the bank about a few cheques. It seemed a very unimportant matter to the young man, but not to his father. Hilary was sent off to Australia immediately. Mr Smith knew little about that place, but he understood one thing. It was a convenient country for people who did not like the customs of old England.

Hilary did not like Australia, and Australia did not like Hilary, so he took the earliest opportunity of returning to England. He could not, of course, earn enough money to buy a ticket, so he had to wait until his father and his brother died. Fortunately, they did this at the same time. After that he received all the money which belonged to the good old family.

There was not a large amount of money, and Hilary soon spent it. (The old family had not been able to earn much in recent years.) When all the money had been spent, Hilary could do one of two things. He could die or work. The thought of neither of these gave him any pleasure. Then he remembered that he was not alone in the world. He had an aunt.

She was his father's only sister, and he knew little about her. His father's old-fashioned ideas were responsible for this unfortunate fact. When she was spoken about, he always looked displeased. "Your aunt Mary behaved very badly. The family name suffered as a result," he said. It seemed that she had failed to marry a lord. Instead, she had chosen a husband who had a small business. Families like the Smiths were too good for that sort of thing, of course. As soon as she became 'Mrs Prothero', she was dead to her brother. Later, Mr Prothero died and left her a lot of money, but that did not bring her back to life in her brother's opinion.

Hilary discovered his aunt's address by talking to the family lawyer. Fortunately, she had continued to use him even after the family turned its back on her. So Hilary's sun shone again, and the old lady seemed to like him. He made frequent visits to his aunt's house; and soon he was living comfortably in the building for which the shopkeeper's money had paid.

Hilary was very happy when he was able to move into the house. He felt like a sailor who had just reached port. He had only about sixpence in his pocket at the time.

One thing was immediately clear: his aunt was seriously ill. She tried not to show it, but she was slowly dying. He had a private talk with her doctor which frightened him greatly. The doctor told him that nothing could cure the old woman. She might live for a little longer, but the end was certain.

'Her condition may become worse at any moment,' the doctor said. 'When it has passed a certain stage, she won't want to live. Nobody with any heart will want her to live either.'

Hilary was very annoyed. Chance had found a home for him, and was now going to throw him out of it. Once again he would have to live alone in the hard world. There was only one thing that he could do. He chose an evening when his aunt was feeling better than usual. Then, very gently, he asked for details of her **will**.

When she heard the word 'will', his aunt laughed loudly.

'Have I made a will?' she said. 'Yes, of course I have. I left all my money to – now, what was it? Who did I leave it to? A religious group in China, I think. Or was it in Polynesia? I can't remember. Blenkinsop, the lawyer, will tell you about it. He still has the will, I expect. I was very religious when I was a girl.'

'Did you make this will when you were a girl, Aunt Mary?'

'Yes, when I was twenty-one. Your grandfather told me to make a will. He believed that everyone should do that. I had no money then, of course, and so there wasn't much point.'

Hilary had been very unhappy when he had heard the first details; but now his eyes were brighter.

'Didn't you make another will when you were married?' he asked.

His aunt shook her head. 'No,' she said. 'There was no need. I had nothing and John had everything. Then, after John died, I had a lot of money but no relations. What could I do with the money?' She looked at Hilary with clear eyes. 'Perhaps I should talk to Mr Blenkinsop again,' she suggested.

Hilary said that there was no need to hurry. Then he changed the subject.

The next day he went to the public library and examined a book which told him what he already believed. When a woman marries, an earlier will is no longer legal. She must make a new will. If no new will is made, the money goes to the nearest relative. Hilary knew that he was his aunt's only relative. His future was safe.

---

will /wɪl/ (n) a legal document saying who should have your property after your death

After a few months had passed, Hilary's financial problems became serious. The change in his aunt's condition showed that the doctor had been right. She went to bed and stayed there. It seemed certain that she would never get up again. At the same time Hilary badly needed money. He had expensive tastes, and a lot of unpaid bills. People were prepared to wait because his aunt was rich; but their bills were high.

Unfortunately, his aunt was now so ill that he could not easily talk to her. She did not want to discuss money matters at all. She was in great pain and found it difficult to sleep, so she became angry when anybody spoke about money. In the end they had an argument about the small amount of ten pounds. She believed that he was trying to get her money, and she said so.

Hilary was not very angry. He understood that Aunt Mary was a sick woman. She was behaving strangely because she was ill. He remembered the doctor's words. Was it kind to want his aunt to live any longer? Would it not be better for her to die now? He thought about this for a long time. When he went to bed, he was still thinking.

In the morning, his aunt told him that she was going to send for Mr Blenkinsop.

So she was going to make a new will! Hilary was not sure that a new will would help him. She might leave all her money to someone else. What could he do then? He reached a decision. He must do the poor old woman a great kindness.

Every night she took some medicine to make her sleep. Hilary decided to double the amount. He did not need to say anything to her about it. He could just put her to sleep for ever.

He found that it was a very easy thing to do. His aunt even made his plans easier. An old servant had been nursing her, and she told this woman to go out. So the servant went off to attend to her own business. She was told to get the medicine ready before she left. Then Hilary could give it to his aunt at the correct time.

It was easy for Hilary. He only had to add more medicine to the glass of water. If anything unexpected happened, he could easily explain. He had not known that the servant had already put the medicine in. So he had put the right

amount into the glass. It was unfortunate, of course. The total amount was too great. But who would ever think that dear Hilary could do anything bad?

His aunt took the glass from his hand with a grateful look.

'Thank you, Hilary,' she said. 'I want, more than anything, to sleep and never to wake up again. That is my greatest wish.' She looked at him and her eyes held his. 'Is that what you wish, Hilary? I have given you your chance. Forgive me if I've got the wrong idea about you. Sick people get these ideas, you know. If I am alive tomorrow, I shall do better for you. Mr Blenkinsop is coming here, and I shall make a will leaving all my money to you. If I die tonight, you'll get nothing. The people in China will get all the money. I should, perhaps, explain. John Prothero never married me. He already had a wife and couldn't marry again. That made your stupid father very angry with me ... No, Hilary, don't try to take the glass away. If you do that, I shall know; and I don't want to know. Good night, Hilary.'

Then, very carefully, she lifted the glass to her lips and drank.

6.1 Were you right?

Look back at your notes in Activity 5.4. Then make true sentences from the table below.

1 Old Mr Smith sends Hilary to Australia because ...

2 Mary's family were ashamed of John Prothero because ...

3 Hilary moves in with his aunt because ...

4 People lend Hilary money because ...

5 Hilary puts too much medicine in his aunt's glass because ...

6 Hilary loses the game because ...

a they know he has a rich aunt who will die soon.

b he owes a lot of money.

c he made his money from running a shop.

d she is very rich.

e he doesn't realise how clever his aunt is.

f he wants to kill her.

6.2 What more did you learn?

Which of these is Aunt Mary thinking in her final moments?

1 There's enough medicine in this glass of water to kill me.

2 I don't want to wake up tomorrow.

3 I'm wrong about Hilary and I'll make a new will tomorrow.

8 I am looking at the face of my murderer.

4 If I die tonight, all my money will go to China.

7 I've tricked him – he can't win!

6 I believe that Hilary loves me.

5 John Prothero was a good husband to me.

5.3 Language in use

Look at the sentence on the right. Then complete these sentences from the story with the right preposition.

> Hilary Smith belonged **to** a good family.

1 Hilary himself had some trouble .... the bank.

2 His father's old-fashioned ideas were responsible .... this unfortunate fact.

3 That did not bring her back .... life, in her brother's opinion.

4 The family turned its back .... her.

5 He had a private talk .... her doctor.

6 The change .... his aunt's condition showed that the doctor had been right.

7 They had an argument about the small amount .... ten pounds.

8 He did not need to say anything to her .... it.

9 His aunt took the glass from his hand .... a grateful look.

10 She lifted the glass .... her lips and drank.

5.4 What's next?

The next story is called *The Birds*. This was made into a very famous film by Alfred Hitchcock.

1 Match the sentences to the pictures.

   a ☐ Birds watch some people eating.

   b ☐ Birds attack to protect young birds.

   c ☐ Birds dive to steal food.

   d ☐ A bird eats from a bird feeder.

2 Which of these situations frightens you? Why? How would you protect yourself? Tell the class.

The Birds

Daphne du Maurier

The smaller birds were at the window now. The larger
birds were attacking the doors.

On December 3rd the wind changed during the night and it was winter. Until then the autumn had been a pleasant one. The leaves had stayed on the trees, golden red, and the earth was rich where the farm workers had turned it.

Nat Hocken, because of a wartime disability, did not work full-time at the farm. He worked three days a week, and they gave him the lighter jobs.

Although he was married with children, he did not much enjoy the company of others, so he preferred to work alone. It pleased him when he was given a gate to mend or a wall to build at the edge of the farm land. Then, at midday, he could look down at the sea and watch the birds while he ate. Autumn was best for this, better than spring. In autumn the birds that stayed to pass the winter came in great **flock**s. They circled in the sky and landed to feed on the rich earth. But even when they fed they seemed to do it without hunger, without desire. Then they returned to the skies again.

Nat watched them, and he watched the seabirds too. Down on the beach they waited for the **tide**. They had more patience, but after feeding they too flocked and circled and cried. Perhaps, thought Nat, a message comes to the birds in autumn. Winter is coming. Many of them will die. People who are worried about an early death force themselves to work or go crazy. Perhaps the birds do the same.

The birds had been more restless than ever this year. As he worked in his fields, the figure of the farmer was lost for a moment in a great cloud of circling, crying birds. There were many more than usual, Nat was sure of this. He said something about it to the farmer when work was finished for the day.

'Yes,' said the farmer, 'there are more birds than usual; I've noticed it, too. And some of them are not even afraid of the machines. I have an idea that the weather will change. It will be a hard winter. That explains the birds' behaviour.'

The farmer was right and it was that night that the temperature suddenly dropped. Nat woke just after two and heard the wind in the chimney. Even the

flock /flɒk/ (n/v) a group of birds
tide /taɪd/ (n) the regular change in the level of the sea

air in the small bedroom had turned cold. Nat pulled the bedclothes round him, moved closer to the back of his sleeping wife, and stayed awake, thoughtful, worried without cause.

Then he heard the **tap**ping on the window. He listened, and the tapping continued. The sound annoyed him, so Nat got out of bed and went to the window. As he opened it, something brushed against his hand, cutting the skin. Then it was gone, over the roof, behind the house. It was a bird of some kind; he could not tell more than that.

He shut the window and went back to bed, but his hand was wet: the cut was bleeding. The bird was frightened, he guessed, and confused. Once more he tried to sleep.

Soon the tapping came again. This time it was more forceful, and now his wife woke at the sound. Turning in the bed, she said to him, 'Check the window, Nat, it's making a noise.'

'I've already checked it,' he told her. 'There's a bird there, trying to get in. Can't you hear the wind? The birds are looking for a place to rest.'

'Send them away,' she said. 'I can't sleep with that noise.'

He went to the window for the second time, and now when he opened it there were a number of birds outside; they flew straight into his face, attacking him.

He shouted, hitting them with his arms. Like the first one, they flew over the roof and disappeared. Quickly he let the window fall and locked it.

'Did you see that?' he said to his wife. 'They attacked me.'

Suddenly a frightened cry came from the children's room.

'It's Jill,' said his wife, sitting up in bed.

There came a second cry of terror, this time from both children. Nat ran into their room and felt the beating of wings all around him in the darkness. The window was wide open. Through it came the birds. First they hit the ceiling and the walls, and then they turned to the children in their beds.

'It's all right, I'm here,' shouted Nat, and the children threw themselves into his arms. In the darkness the birds flew up and turned to attack again.

'What is it, Nat, what's happened?' his wife called. He quickly pushed the children outside and shut the door behind them. He was alone now, in their bedroom, with the birds.

He fought with them in the darkness for a long time, but at last the beating of the wings around him stopped. He waited, listened; there was no sound except the crying of one of the children.

tap /tæp/ (v) to knock gently against something hard

He looked around him. The living birds had gone; the dead lay on the floor. Nat looked down, shocked, at the little bodies. There were at least fifty of them lying there on the floor. They had destroyed themselves against the bedroom walls, or had been destroyed by him in the fight.

Nat shut the window and the door of the small bedroom, and went back to his own room. His wife was sitting up in bed, one child asleep beside her, the smaller one in her arms. She shook her head as a sign for him to be silent.

'He's sleeping now,' she whispered, 'but only just. There was blood on his face. Jill said that it was the birds. She woke up, and the birds were in the room.'

His wife looked up at Nat, frightened and confused. He did not want her to know that he was also very worried about the events of the past few hours.

He sat down on the bed beside his wife, and held her hand. 'It's the weather,' he said, 'the cold weather.'

'But Nat,' his wife whispered, 'it's only last night that the weather changed. And they can't be hungry yet. There's food for them out there in the fields.'

They looked at one another for a while without speaking.

'I'll go downstairs and make a cup of tea,' he said.

He drank his tea in the kitchen, and carried a cup up to his wife. Then he washed, put on his boots and opened the back door.

The sky was dark, and the ground was frozen hard. He had never known a change so quick and sudden. Black winter had arrived in a single night.

The children were awake now, and soon they came down to breakfast.

'Did you drive away the birds?' asked Jill.

'Yes, they've all gone now,' said Nat. 'The wind brought them in. They were frightened and lost.'

'I hope they won't come again,' said Jill. 'They tried to hurt us. Perhaps if we put bread for them outside the window they will eat that and fly away.'

She finished her breakfast and then went for her coat and her school books. Nat said nothing, but his wife looked at him across the table. A silent message passed between them.

'I'll walk with her to the bus,' he said. 'I'm not working today.'

After the bus left, Nat walked back towards the farm. Jim, the cowman, was there.

'Is the boss around?' asked Nat.

'He's gone to market,' said Jim. 'It's Tuesday, isn't it?'

'Have you had any trouble with the birds?' asked Nat.

'Birds? What birds?'

'We got them in our place last night. Lots of them came in the children's bedroom. Frightened them.'

'Cold, perhaps. Hungry. You put out some bread for them.'

Jim was not interested. Nat walked back home. His wife was in the kitchen with young Johnny.

'Did you see anyone?' she asked.

'Jim,' he answered. 'I don't think he believed me. There's nothing wrong up there.'

'Can you take the dead birds away?' she asked. 'I need to make the beds.'

He went up with a large bag and dropped the bodies into it, one by one. He took the bag out into the garden and was faced now with a new problem. The ground was too hard to dig. But nothing had happened in the past hours except the coming of the east wind. It was unnatural.

He decided to take the birds to the beach and dig a hole for them. When he reached the beach, it was difficult to stand against the force of the east wind. His hands were blue. He had never known such cold, not in all the bad winters he could remember. The sea was out. He dug a hole in the sand for the birds. But as he opened the bag, the wind carried them, lifted them, and blew them away from him along the beach.

'The tide will take them when it turns,' he said to himself.

Then he saw them. The **gull**s. Out there, riding the sea.

Hundreds, thousands, tens of thousands ... They were sitting on the waves, heads to the wind, waiting for the tide. To the east, and to the west, the gulls were there. They stretched as far as his eye could reach.

Nat turned, and climbed the steep path home. Someone should know of this. He should tell someone. Something was happening, because of the east wind and the weather, that he did not understand. He thought about ringing the police from the phone box by the bus stop. But what could they do? What could anyone do? Tens of thousands of gulls riding the sea out there, because of the cold, because of hunger.

gull /gʌl/ (n) a grey and white bird that lives near the sea

As Nat came near to the house, his wife met him at the door.

'Nat,' she said, 'it's on the radio.'

'What's on the radio?' he asked.

'About the birds. It's not only here, it's everywhere. In London, and other cities, and all over the country. Something has happened to the birds.'

'Let's hope they'll hear that at the farm,' he said. 'It's true. All over the country. I've been telling myself all morning that there's something wrong. And just now, down on the beach, I looked out to sea. There are gulls, thousands of them, tens of thousands. They're all out there, waiting.'

'What are they waiting for, Nat?' she asked.

'I don't know,' he said slowly. 'But I'm going to cover the windows and chimneys.'

He went upstairs and worked there for the rest of the morning. He boarded the bedroom windows and filled up the bottoms of the chimneys.

'Dinner's ready.' His wife called him from the kitchen.

'All right. I'm coming down.'

'How much food have we got?' he asked his wife when they had eaten.

'It's shopping day tomorrow, you know that.'

Nat did not want to frighten her. He thought that she might not be able to go into town tomorrow. He looked in the cupboards. There was enough for two or three days. Not much bread, though.

'What about the baker?'

'He comes tomorrow, too.'

He saw that she had flour. If the baker did not call, she had enough to bake one loaf.

Nat fixed boards across the kitchen windows. Then he went out of the back door and stood in the garden, looking down towards the sea. There had been no sun all day, and now, even before three o'clock, a kind of darkness had already come. He walked down the path, halfway to the beach. And then he stopped. The gulls were circling, hundreds of them, thousands of them. The gulls were making the sky dark. And they were completely silent.

Nat turned. He ran up the path, back to the house.

'I'm going for Jill,' he told his wife. 'I'll wait for her at the bus stop.'

'What's the matter?' asked his wife. 'You've gone quite white.'

'Keep Johnny inside,' he said. 'Keep the door shut and close the curtains.'

'It's only just after three,' she said.

'Just do what I tell you.'

He picked up a heavy stick. Then he started walking to the bus stop, and now and again he looked back over his shoulder.

The gulls had flown higher now. Their circles were wider; they were spreading out across the sky.

At the top of the hill he waited. There was still half an hour until the bus arrived. In the distance he could see the hills, white and clean against the darkness of the sky. Something black came from behind them, and became a cloud. The cloud divided again into other clouds, spreading north, east, south and west. They were not clouds at all; they were birds. He watched them travel across the sky. As one flock passed over, only sixty or seventy metres above him, he knew from their speed that they were flying inland.

'They've been given the towns,' thought Nat. 'We don't matter so much here. The gulls are enough.'

The bus came up the hill. Jill climbed out, and three or four other children. They crowded around him, laughing.

'Come on now, let's get home,' he said. 'It's cold. Here, you. I'll watch you across the fields. Run as fast as you can.'

He was speaking to Jill's friends.

'We want to play for a bit out here,' said one of them.

'No, you don't. You go straight home.'

They whispered to one another, then ran off across the fields. Jill looked at her father.

'We always play after school,' she said.

'Not tonight,' he said.

He could see the gulls now. They were circling the fields, coming in towards the land. Still silent.

'Look, look at all the gulls.'

'Yes. Hurry, now.'

'Where are they going?'

'Somewhere warmer, I expect.'

'What is it? What are the gulls doing? I don't like them. They're coming closer.'

He started running, holding Jill's hand. As they went past the farm turning, he saw the farmer in his car. Nat called to him.

'Can you give us a lift?' he said.

'What's that?' Mr Trigg, the farmer, turned in the driving seat and looked at them. Then a smile came to his cheerful face.

'Have you seen the gulls?' he said. 'Jim and I are going to try shooting at them. Do you want a gun?'

Nat shook his head. 'I don't want a gun. Would you drive Jill home? She's frightened of the birds.'

'OK,' said the farmer, 'I'll take her home. Why don't you stay and shoot with us? We'll frighten them away.'

Jill climbed in. There was no room for Nat, so he followed the car on foot. 'What use is a gun,' he thought, 'against a sky of birds?'

They were coming in towards the farm. They were circling lower in the sky. Nat walked faster towards his own house. He saw the farmer's car returning.

'The child has run inside,' said the farmer. 'Your wife was watching for her. Well, will you join us now?'

'No, I'll go home. Or my wife will be worried. Have you boarded your windows?'

'No. What for? They don't frighten me.'

'I'd board them now, if I were you.'

'Perhaps. See you in the morning. I'll give you a gull breakfast.'

Nat hurried on. Past the little wood, and then across the field.

He heard the sound of wings above him. A gull flew at him from the sky, missed, and circled again. In a moment it was joined by others, six, seven, ten. Nat dropped his stick; it was useless. Covering his head with his arms, he ran towards the house. They kept coming at him from the air, silent except for the beating wings. He could feel the blood on his hands, his arms, his neck. He fought to keep them from his eyes. Nothing else mattered. They had no thought for themselves. When they missed, they crashed to the ground. As Nat ran, he kicked their dead bodies in front of him. He found the door, opened it and fell inside.

His wife washed his cuts. They were not deep. The children were crying. They had seen the blood on their father's hands.

'It's all right now,' he told them. 'I'm not hurt.'

His wife was white.

'Why don't they do something? Why don't they get the army, get guns, anything?'

'There's been no time. Nobody's prepared. We'll listen to the six o'clock news.'

Nat went back into the kitchen, followed by his wife. Johnny was playing quietly on the floor. Only Jill looked anxious.

'I can hear the birds,' she said.

Nat listened. There were sounds at the windows, at the door. Wings were moving against the surface, looking for a way in. Now and again came a crash; a bird had attacked and fallen. 'Some of them will kill themselves that way,' he thought, 'but not enough. Never enough.'

'It's all right,' he said to his daughter. 'I've got boards over the windows, Jill. The birds can't get in.'

He decided that they must sleep in the kitchen and keep the fire burning. He was afraid of the bedroom chimneys. The boards that he had placed at the bottom of the chimneys might break. In the kitchen they were safe, because the fire would keep the birds out of the chimney. If the worst happened, the birds could not get out of the bedrooms. They could do no harm there.

'We're safe enough now,' he thought, as he brought the bedclothes down. 'It's just the food that worries me. Food, and wood for the fire. We've enough for two or three days, not more.'

He turned the radio on.

'This is London,' the announcer said. 'The government is doing its best to protect the lives and property of the population, but asks everyone to stay indoors tonight. The birds are attacking anyone on sight, and they have already begun to attack buildings. The population is asked to stay calm.'

The sound died. Nat turned off the radio. He looked at his wife. She looked back at him.

'What does it mean?' said Jill. 'What did the news say?'

'There won't be any more programmes tonight,' said Nat. 'We'll have supper early.' He wanted the look of fear to go from Jill's face.

He helped with the supper, and then he went up to the bedrooms and listened. He no longer heard the beating of wings on the roof.

'They know that it's hard to break in here,' he thought. 'They'll go away again.'

After supper, when they were clearing away, they heard a new, familiar sound.

His wife looked up at him, smiling. 'It's planes,' she said. 'They're sending out planes after the birds. Isn't that gunfire? Can't you hear guns?'

Just then they heard a crash about three kilometres away. It was followed by a second, and then a third.

'What was that?' asked his wife. 'Were they dropping bombs on the birds?'

'I don't know,' answered Nat. 'I don't think so.'

He did not want to tell her that the sound was the crashing of planes. What could planes do against birds that threw themselves at them? The whole idea was crazy.

'Where have the planes gone?' asked Jill.

'Back home,' he said. 'Come on now, time for bed.'

His wife undressed the children in front of the fire while he checked the house again.

He looked at his watch. Nearly eight o'clock. It was high water an hour ago. That explained the silence; the birds attacked with the flood tide. It might not work that way inland, but this seemed to be the way on the coast. So they had six hours without attack. When the tide turned again, at about 1.20 in the morning, the birds would come back ...

The children were asleep. Softly, he opened the back door and looked out.

It was black out there. The wind was blowing harder than ever, icy, from the sea. There were dead birds everywhere. Under the broken windows, against the wall. The living had flown out to sea with the turn of the tide.

Only the boards had stopped the birds from coming in.

He went inside again, lay down and closed his eyes. His wife finally woke him, shaking his shoulder.

'They've begun,' she cried. 'They started an hour ago, I can't listen to it alone any longer. Something smells bad too; something is burning.'

Then he remembered. He had forgotten to put more wood on the fire. It was nearly out. He got up quickly. The tapping had started on the windows and the doors, but he took no notice. He knew what the burning smell was. The birds were coming down the chimney, and dropping into the dying fire.

He got sticks and paper and put them on the fire. Then he reached for the can of petrol.

'Stand back,' he shouted to his wife. He threw the petrol on the fire. The flame shot up the chimney, and the burnt bodies of the birds fell down into the fire.

The children woke, crying. 'What is it?' asked Jill. 'What's happened?'

'Stop crying,' he called to the children. 'There's nothing to be afraid of.'

Three in the morning. Another four or five hours before high water.

'Make us some tea,' he said to his wife. 'We can't sit around doing nothing.'

Keep her busy, and the children, too. Move around, eat, drink.

He waited by the fire. No more bodies fell from the chimney. There were no birds up there now.

'Come on now, Jill,' he said, 'bring me some more sticks.'

The danger from the chimney was over. It could not happen again, not if he kept the fire burning day and night.

'I'll have to get more petrol from the farm tomorrow,' he thought.

While the tapping continued at the windows, he sat with one arm around his wife and the other round Jill. Johnny sat on his mother's knees.

At 5.30 he suggested breakfast to calm the frightened children. He found himself watching the clock. If the attack did not stop with the turn of the tide, they were beaten. They could not continue through the long day without air, without rest, without more petrol, without ...

His wife's voice drove away the sudden desire for sleep.

'What is it? What now?' he said.

'It's getting light,' whispered his wife. 'I can't see it, but I can feel it. And the birds aren't so loud.'

She was right. The tide was turning. By eight there was no sound at all. Only the wind. The children finally fell asleep.

He went outside, kicking the bodies from the step, and he breathed the cold air. He had six working hours before him. Food, and light, and fuel; these were the necessary things.

He stepped into the garden, and there he saw the living birds. The gulls had gone back to ride the sea; they were looking for sea food before they returned to the attack. But the land birds waited and watched.

He went to the end of the garden. The birds did not move. They continued watching him.

'I've got to get food,' Nat said to himself. 'I've got to get to the farm and find food.'

He went back to the house. He checked the windows and the doors. Then he went to speak to his wife.

'I'm going to the farm,' he said.

She held him. She had seen the living birds from the open door.

'Take us with you,' she asked. 'We can't stay here alone.'

He considered the matter and then agreed.

'Bring some bags, then,' he said.

His wife carried Johnny. Nat took Jill's hand.

'The birds,' she whispered, 'they're all out there, in the fields.'

'They won't hurt us,' he said, 'not in the light.'

They started walking across the field, and the birds did not move. They waited, their heads turned to the wind.

At the entrance to the farm, Nat told his wife to wait with the two children.

'But I want to see Mrs Trigg,' she said. 'There are a lot of things that we can borrow—'

'Wait here,' Nat interrupted, 'I'll be back in a moment.'

He went down alone to the farm. He saw the car standing by the gate, not in the garage. The windows of the farmhouse were broken. There were dead gulls lying around the house. The living birds sat, quite still, on the trees behind the farm and on the roof of the house.

Jim's body lay outside. His gun was beside him. The door of the house was locked, but Nat lifted a window and climbed through. Trigg's body was close to the telephone. No sign of Mrs Trigg. Upstairs, perhaps.

'Thank God,' he said to himself, 'there were no children.'

He forced himself to climb the stairs, but halfway up he turned and went down again. He could see her legs, in the bedroom doorway. Beside her were the bodies of the gulls and a broken stick.

'I can't do anything for them,' thought Nat. 'I've got less than five hours.'

He returned to his wife and children.

'I'm going to fill up their car,' he said. 'I'll put wood in it and petrol. We'll take it home and return for more.'

'What about the Triggs?' asked his wife.

'They're probably with friends,' he said.

'Shall I come and help you, then?'

'No; stay here. I'll get the car. You can sit in it.'

He backed the car out into the road. His wife and children could not see Jim's body from there.

'Stay here,' he said.

Her eyes watched his all the time. He believed that she understood.

They made three journeys, backwards and forwards between their house and the farm. Then he was satisfied that they had everything. It was surprising how many things were necessary. New boards for the windows. Petrol, firewood, canned food; the list was endless. He milked three of the cows.

On the final journey he drove the car to the bus stop, and walked across to the phone box. He tried several times, but the line was dead. He looked out over the countryside, but there was no sign of life at all. There was nothing in the fields except the waiting, watching birds.

'Why aren't they feeding?' he asked himself.

Then he remembered. They had eaten during the night.

He thought of the children who had run across the fields the night before. No smoke came from the chimneys of their houses.

He went back to the car and got into the driver's seat.

'Go quickly past that second gate,' whispered his wife. 'The postman's lying there. I don't want Jill to see.'

It was a quarter to one when they reached the house. Only one more hour.

Nat carried everything inside the house. They could organize it later, during the long hours ahead. First he must check the windows and the doors.

He went round the house, testing every window, every door. He climbed on the roof, and fixed boards across every chimney, except the kitchen one. The cold was terrible, but he had to do the job. Now and again he looked up, hoping for planes. There was enough time. But none came.

'It's always the same,' he said to himself. 'No plan, no organization. And we don't matter, down here in the country.'

He paused when his work on the bedroom chimney was finished, and looked out to sea. Something was moving out there.

'Ah, ships!' he said. 'They're going to protect us from the sea.'

He waited, his eyes watering in the wind. He was wrong, though. It was not ships. The gulls were coming. The tide had turned again.

Nat climbed down the ladder and went inside. The family were in the kitchen having dinner. It was a little after two. He locked the door.

'It's night-time,' said young Johnny.

His wife turned on the radio, but no sound came from it.

'I've tried everything,' she said, 'even foreign stations. I can't get anything.'

'Perhaps they have the same trouble,' he said. 'Perhaps it's the same all across Europe.'

They ate in silence.

The tapping began at the windows, at the doors. The first crash of a gull on the step.

'Won't America do something?' said his wife. 'They've always been our friends, haven't they? Surely America will do something?'

Nat did not answer. The boards were strong against the windows, and on the chimneys, too. The house was filled with stores, with wood. They had everything that they needed for the next few days. His wife could help him put them away, and the children, too. They'd work between now and a quarter to nine, when the tide would go out again; then they could sleep until three in the morning.

The smaller birds were at the window now. He recognized their light tapping, and the soft movement of their wings. The larger birds were attacking the doors. Nat listened to the sound of the breaking wood. He asked himself how many millions of years of memory were stored in those little brains. What was it in those brains that had given them this desire to destroy humans as effortlessly as machines?

1 **Write answers to these questions.**

Which story:
- is the most frightening? ....
- is the funniest? ....
- did you like best? ....
- did you like least? ....

Talk to other students. Discuss the reasons for your choices. Do you all agree?

2 **Look at these characters from the book. Work with a partner and choose a character each. Describe your character to your partner. Say what the person looks like, what kind of person they are and what part they played in the story.**

3 **Work in groups of three or four.**

Student A:	Think of a character from the book. Don't tell the others who you are thinking of. Answer questions with the words *yes* and *no* only.
Students B–D:	Ask yes/no questions (for example, *Is it a man?*) to find out which character your friend is thinking of. How few questions do you need before you guess correctly?

1 **Short stories often end very suddenly. Sometimes we want to know more. Choose one of the stories in this book. Describe what happened next.**

> Will the birds kill everyone on Earth?

> Does Mr Beaseley find out what happened to his wife?

> Does Jeepo and Homer's company succeed?

....

....

....

....

....

....

....

....

....

Choose a picture from page 5, page 42, page 50 or page 61. Write a description of what has just happened, what is happening now and what is going to happen. Include conversation if you like.

....

....

....

....

....

....

....

....

....

Work with other students. You are a new film company. Your first project is to make a short, 20-minute film of *The Birds*.

1 Choose a name for your film company.

Name

2 Prepare the story. Read this part of a film story for *It Happened Near a Lake*. Then work with the other students in your film company. Make notes for a film story for *The Birds*. Choose five important scenes.

Scene 1   a 1950s kitchen in a small American town; Mr Beaseley sits at the table opening his post; he calmly tells his nasty wife that someone has left him $400,000.

Scene 2   to show that they have travelled a lot, several travel advertisements pass by Mr and Mrs Beaseley as they stand with their suitcases: the Andes, the Yucatan, Buenos Aires.

Scene 3   a comfortable hotel in Buenos Aires: the arrival area; Mr Beaseley talks to a Portuguese doctor (both are dressed in white suits) over a cup of coffee; they plan a trip up the River Amazon to see a terrible monster.

Opening title scene

Scene 1

Scene 2

Scene 3

Scene 4

Scene 5

Choose your actors, from anywhere in the world. Try to find photos to show the class. Here are your characters:

Nat Hocken, the father	
Nat's wife (who has no name in the story, so give her a name)	
Jill and Johnny	
Mr and Mrs Trigg	
Jim, the cowman	

Choose a place to film.
The story takes place by the sea. This is important because the gulls come and go as the sea goes in and out. This gives the family time to collect wood, food and petrol.
Each member of your group should suggest somewhere to film.
Then vote on the best idea.

Place to film

Choose your music. The music is going to be very important. Use it to change the mood, and to build up the feeling of terror towards the end.

Opening music	
Scene 1	
Scene 2	
Scene 3	
Scene 4	
Scene 5	
Closing music	

Think of a clever line to advertise your film. Alfred Hitchcock advertised his 1963 film of *The Birds* like this: *The Birds* are coming ... .

Advertising idea

Present your film plan to your class. Whose film sounds best?

8 Choose your favourite scene from your film plan. Write the words for the actors. Choose people in your group to act the different parts. Add new parts if there are too many of you. Practise the scene and act it out for your class.